LATIN'S NOT SO TOUGH!

LEVEL TWO ANSWER KEY

A Classical Latin Worktext
by
Karen Mohs

Dear Parent/Teacher:

This answer key is designed to assist you in teaching Latin Workbook Level Two.

Daily flashcard practice is essential. Please do not neglect this effective learning tool. The letters and words for flashcard use are located at the end of the workbook.

Most importantly, continue to make this an enjoyable learning experience and a happy memory for both you and your student.

References for this series include *First Year Latin* by Charles Jenney, Jr., *Second Year Latin* by Charles Jenney, Jr., and *The New College Latin & English Dictionary* by John C. Traupman, Ph.D.

Copyright © 1997 by Karen Mohs
All rights reserved. No part of this publication may be reproduced without prior permission of the author.

ISBN-13: 978-1-931842-56-3
ISBN-10: 1-931842-56-6

Greek 'n' Stuff
P.O. Box 882
Moline, IL 61266-0882
www.greeknstuff.com

SCHEDULE OF LESSONS
(PROPOSAL FOR LEVEL TWO)

In overview, the *Latin's Not So Tough!* workbooks are designed such that the student ideally completes one page per day (and practices his or her flashcards each day as well). (It should be noted that older students often complete more than one page per day when they are working in the early levels.) The workbooks were not designed within a framework of "lessons." Many parents have told us they appreciate this approach. It is easy to follow, without need of additional parent/teacher preparation and scheduling.

However, some parents/teachers prefer the "lesson" approach. Please be aware that this "Schedule of Lessons" is an artificial grid placed over a series not written with this grid in mind. The assigned pages are arbitrary and should be modified so the student can progress through the workbooks at a pace suitable to his or her age/skill level.

A note about our methodology:
    Referred to by some as the "Saxon of Latin," this series begins gently and advances gradually, providing plenty of reinforcement through a wide variety of workbook activities and translation exercises. By introducing new concepts slowly, *Latin's Not So Tough!* avoids the pitfall common to many foreign language courses whereby the student suddenly faces a steep learning curve, becomes frustrated, fails to internalize the language, and develops an aversion to foreign language study in general. The overwhelming response from those using *Latin's Not So Tough!* can be summed up by the words we hear so often: "This is my student's favorite subject."

Lesson 1
Pages 1-6 - Alphabet review - Part 1

Teacher tip:
    Latin's Not So Tough! teaches classical pronunciation. Because the distinctions between classical and ecclesiastical pronunciations are relatively minor, students generally do not find it difficult to switch from one pronunciation to another. For a comparison of the classical and ecclesiastical pronunciations, see pages 4-6 of *The New College Latin & English Dictionary* by John C. Traupman, Ph.D. For a thorough examination of pronunciation, see pages 1-8 of *New Latin Grammar* by Charles E. Bennett or pages 1-6 of *Latin Grammar* by B.L. Gildersleeve & G. Lodge.

Lesson 2
Pages 7-11 - Alphabet review - Part 2

Lesson 3
    Pages 12-14 - Diphthong review

Lesson 4
    Pages 15-20 - Special Consonants review

Lesson 5
    Pages 21-24 - New vocabulary - **puella** and **vocō**, vocabulary practice

Teacher tip:
    Use the derivatives to help your student learn the vocabulary. One parent using this series chooses a derivative and has her students write that derivative as a hint in the large box in which the Latin vocabulary word is first taught. For example, when she teaches "**ager**," she has her students write "agriculture" in the box. If the word does not have an English derivative, such as "**pugnō**," she thinks of a silly saying, such as "The **pug** dog likes to fight." Other parents point out derivatives encountered in daily activities and have their students attempt to recall the Latin vocabulary words from which the English words come. Many such techniques are helpful in reinforcing the vocabulary.

    As is generally true when translating from one language into another, a particular Latin word can often have a range of English meanings. To discern the correct choice, translators rely on context. However, your student is just beginning to learn Latin. At this point in his studies, he is encountering words in isolation. Without context, he has no basis for knowing which words most closely render the original author's meaning. Any of the possible answers should be considered correct.

English derivatives:
    vocō (vocabulary, vocation, avocation, advocate, convoke, revoke, invoke, evoke, provoke, vocable)

Lesson 6
    Pages 25-28 - New vocabulary - **puer** and **dō**, vocabulary practice

English derivatives:
    puer (puerile, puerilely, puerileness, puerilism, puerility, puerperium)
    dō (date, datum, dative, edition, tradition, perdition, add, dado, dice)

Lesson 7
Pages 29-32 - New vocabulary - **agricola** and **aqua**, vocabulary practice

> *English derivatives:*
> aqua (aqua, aquarium, aqueduct, aqueous, aquamarine, aquatic, semiaquatic, aquatint, aquacade, aquanaut, aquaplane, aquarelle, Aquarius, gouache, ewer)

Lesson 8
Pages 33-36 - New vocabulary - **est** and **fēmina**, vocabulary practice

> *English derivatives:*
> fēmina (female, feminine, effeminate, femininity, femme, feme)

****
QUIZ #1 (optional)
****

Lesson 9
Pages 37-40 - New vocabulary - **et** and **silva**, vocabulary practice

> *English derivatives:*
> silva (silva, sylvan, savage, selva, silvichemical, silvicolous, silviculture, sylph, sylvatic)

Lesson 10
Pages 41-42 - Vocabulary practice - Part 1

Lesson 11
Pages 43-46 - New vocabulary - **īnsula** and **sunt**, vocabulary practice

> *English derivatives:*
> īnsula (isle, peninsula, isolate, isolation, insulate, insular)

Lesson 12
Pages 47-50 - New vocabulary - **laudō** and **nōn**, vocabulary practice

> *English derivatives:*
> laudō (laud, laudable, laudatory, allow)

Lesson 13
Pages 51-54 - New vocabulary - **ad** and **vīta**, vocabulary practice

> *English derivatives:*
> vīta (vita, vital, vitality, vitamin, revitalize, devitalize, viable)

Lesson 14
Pages 55-58 - New vocabulary - **porta** and **memoria**, vocabulary practice

> *English derivatives:*
> **porta** (porter, portal, portico, porch, portcullis, porthole)
> **memoria** (memorial, memory, memoir, memorize, memorable, memorandum)

Lesson 15
Pages 59-62 - New vocabulary - **nāvigō** and **sed**, vocabulary practice

> *English derivatives:*
> **nāvigō** (navy, navigate, navigation, navigable)

Lesson 16
Pages 63-64 - Vocabulary practice - Part 2

Lesson 17
Pages 65-68 - New vocabulary - **fortūna** and **via**, vocabulary practice

> *English derivatives:*
> **fortūna** (fortune, fortunate, fortunately, unfortunate)
> **via** (via, viatic, viaduct, trivial, trivium, quadrivium, envoy, previous, pervious, impervious, obvious, devious, deviate, voyage, convey)

Lesson 18
Pages 69-72 - New vocabulary - **portō** and **quid**, vocabulary practice

> *English derivatives:*
> **portō** (portfolio, porter, portable, rapport, deport, disport, export, purport, comport, import, transport, support, report, portage, portamento, portative)
> **quid** (quidnunc, quiddity, quip)

```
************
QUIZ #2 (optional)
************
```

```
******************
MIDTERM EXAM (optional)
******************
```

Lesson 19
Page 73-76 - New vocabulary - **tuba** and **ager**, vocabulary practice

> *English derivatives:*
> **tuba** (tuba, tubaist, tubist, saxtuba)
> **ager** (agriculture, agrarian, peregrine, pilgrim, agronomy)

Lesson 20
    Pages 77-80 - New vocabulary - parō and amīcus, vocabulary practice

> *English derivatives:*
>   parō (parasol, rampart, emperor, disparate, pare, apparatus, prepare, repair, parade, separate, parapet, parachute, parador, parlay, parry, parament)
>   amīcus (amigo, amity, amicable, amiable, amiably, amiability)

Lesson 21
    Pages 81-84 - New vocabulary - spectō and nātūra, vocabulary practice

> *English derivatives:*
>   spectō (spectator, spectacle, bespectacled, speculate, expect, aspect, respect, inspect, prospect, suspect, circumspect)
>   nātūra (nature, natural, supernatural, preternatural)

Lesson 22
    Pages 85-86 - Vocabulary practice - Part 3

Lesson 23
    Pages 87-90 - New vocabulary - campus and occupō, vocabulary practice

> *English derivatives:*
>   campus (campus, camp, campaign, champion, scamper, campo, campestral, campesino, champerty)
>   occupō (occupation, occupy)

Lesson 24
    Pages 91-94 - New vocabulary - cum and nauta, vocabulary practice

> *English derivatives:*
>   nauta (nautical)

Lesson 25
    Pages 95-98 - New vocabulary - vīlla and littera, vocabulary practice

> *English derivatives:*
>   vīlla (villa, village, villain, villanelle)
>   littera (literal, literary, literate, illiterate, alliteration, transliterate, obliterate, letter, literatim)

Lesson 26
    Page 99-102 - New vocabulary - **ubi** and **filius**, vocabulary practice

> *English derivatives:*
>   ubi (ubiquity, ubiety, alibi)
>   filius (filial, filiate, affiliate)

Lesson 27
    Page 103-106 - New vocabulary - **patria** and **filia**, vocabulary practice

> *English derivatives:*
>   patria (repatriate, expatriate, patriarch)

Lesson 28
    Pages 107-108 - Vocabulary practice - Part 4

```
***********
QUIZ #3 (optional)
***********
```

Lesson 29
    Pages 109-112 - New vocabulary - **amīcitia** and **amō**, vocabulary practice

> *English derivatives:*
>   amō (amorous, amateur, amative, paramour, inamorato, amatory)

Lesson 30
    Pages 113-116 - New vocabulary - **lingua** and **equus**, vocabulary practice

> *English derivatives:*
>   lingua (lingua, language, linguist, linguistics, bilingual, lingo,
>   linguine, lingulate, languet)
>   equus (equine, equestrian, equitant, equisetum)

Lesson 31
    Pages 117-120 - New vocabulary - **poēta** and **annus**, vocabulary practice

> *English derivatives:*
>   poēta (poet, poetry, poetical, poetaster)
>   annus (annual, annals, anniversary, millenium, annuity,
>   superannuated, perennial, biennium, triennium)

Lesson 32
    Pages 121-124 - New vocabulary - pugnō and terra, vocabulary practice

> *English derivatives:*
>   pugnō (pugnacious, repugn, inexpugnable, oppugn, impugn)
>   terra (terra, terra cotta, terrier, terrarium, territory, terrace, inter, tureen, mediterranean, subterranean, terrestrial, terrene, terreplein, parterre, terraqueous, terrigenous, terricolous)

Lesson 33
    Page 125-128 - New vocabulary - gladius and prōvincia, vocabulary practice

> *English derivatives:*
>   gladius (gladiator, gladiate, gladiolus, glaive)
>   prōvincia (province, provincial, provincialize)

Lesson 34
    Page 129-134 - Vocabulary practice - Part 5

Lesson 35
    Page 135-139 - Final review - Part 1

Lesson 36
    Page 140-144 - Final review - Part 2

    ****
    QUIZ #4 (optional)
    ****

    ****
    FINAL EXAM (optional)
    ****

Appendix

Latin - English Glossary	145
English - Latin Glossary	146
Latin Alphabet	147
Special Sounds	147
Flashcard Tips	148

Lesson 1

LET'S REVIEW THE LATIN ALPHABET

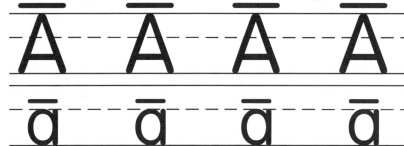

As you write the letters across each line, say the sound of "**a**" in *father*.

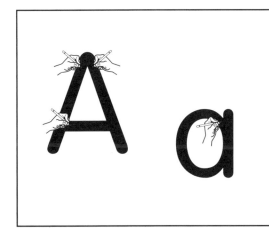

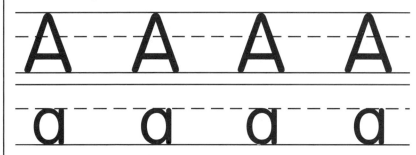

As you write the letters across each line, say the sound of "**a**" in *idea*.

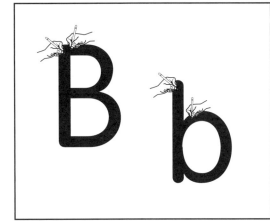

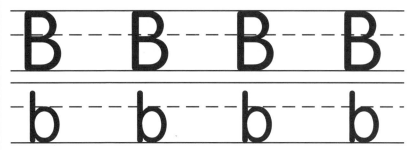

As you write the letters across each line, say the sound of "**b**" in *boy*.

Start your flashcard deck with these cards. Review them every day.
(See back of workbook.)
☐ I practiced my flashcards today.

Latin Workbook - Level 2
Copyright © 1997 by Karen Mohs

MORE ALPHABET REVIEW

As you write the letters across each line, say the sound of "**c**" in *cat*.

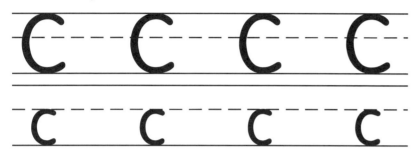
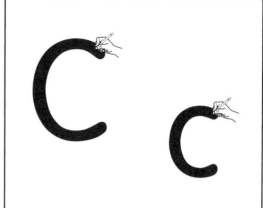

As you write the letters across each line, say the sound of "**d**" in *dog*.

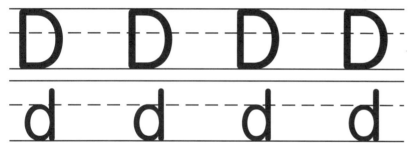

As you write the letters across each line, say the sound of "**ey**" in *obey*.

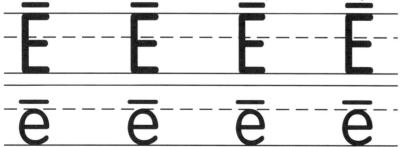
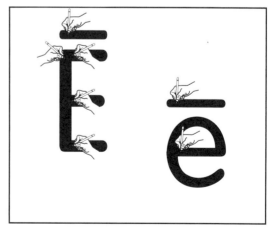

☐ I practiced my flashcards today. (Add the new cards.)

MORE ALPHABET REVIEW

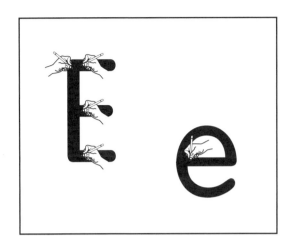

As you write the letters across each line, say the sound of "**e**" in *bet*.

As you write the letters across each line, say the sound of "**f**" in *fan*.

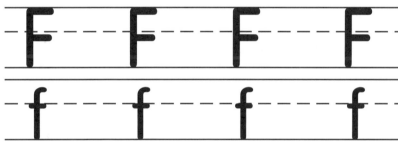

As you write the letters across each line, say the sound of "**g**" in *go*.

☐ I practiced my flashcards today. (Add the new cards.)

MORE ALPHABET REVIEW

As you write the letters across each line, say the sound of "**h**" in *hat*.

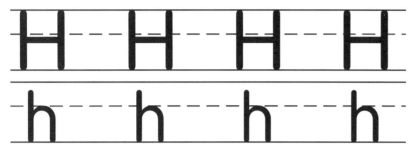

As you write the letters across each line, say the sound of "**ī**" in *machine*.

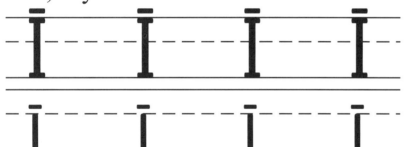
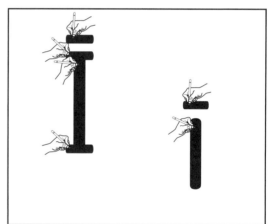

As you write the letters across each line, say the sound of "**i**" in *sit*.

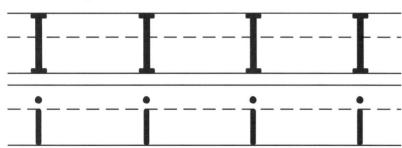
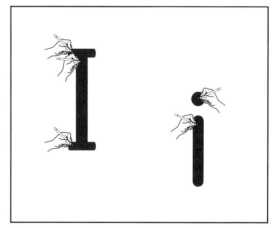

☐ I practiced my flashcards today. (Add the new cards.)

MORE ALPHABET REVIEW

As you write the letters across each line, say the sound of "**k**" in *king*.

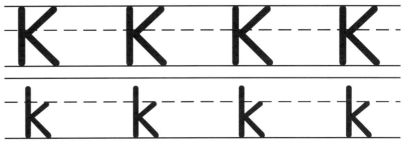

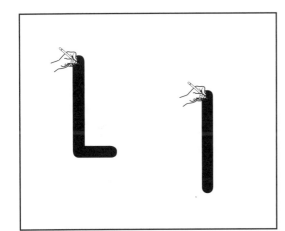

As you write the letters across each line, say the sound of "**l**" in *land*.

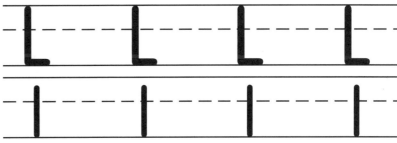

As you write the letters across each line, say the sound of "**m**" in *man*.

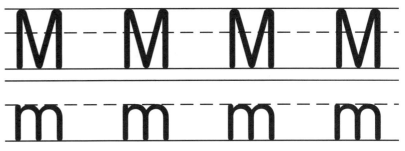

☐ I practiced my flashcards today. (Add the new cards.)

MORE ALPHABET REVIEW

As you write the letters across each line, say the sound of "**n**" in *nut*.

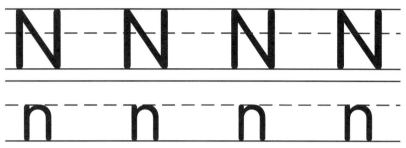

As you write the letters across each line, say the sound of "**o**" in *note*.*

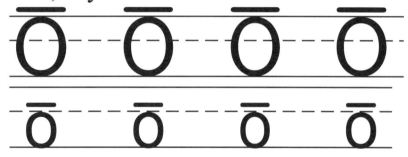

As you write the letters across each line, say the sound of "**o**" in *omit*.*

*Although both Latin "o" sounds are "long," the ō as in *note* is held longer than the o as in *omit*.

☐ I practiced my flashcards today. (Add the new cards.)

MORE ALPHABET REVIEW

As you write the letters across each line, say the sound of "**p**" in *pit*.

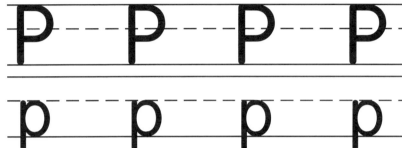

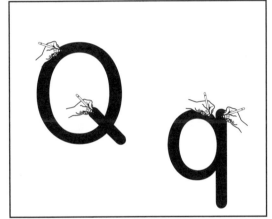

As you write the letters across each line, say the sound of "**qu**" in *quit*.

As you write the letters across each line, say the sound of "**r**" in *run*.

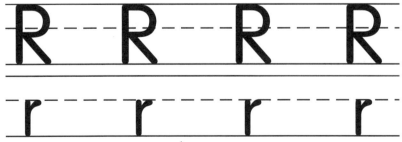

☐ I practiced my flashcards today. (Add the new cards.)

MORE ALPHABET REVIEW

As you write the letters across each line, say the sound of "**s**" in *sit*.

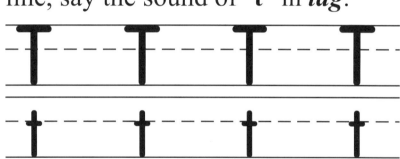
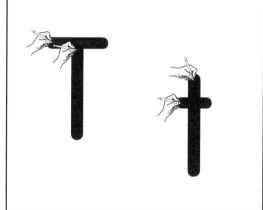

As you write the letters across each line, say the sound of "**t**" in *tag*.

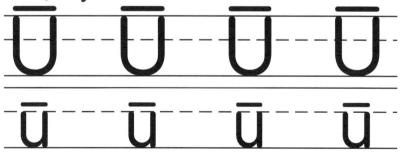

As you write the letters across each line, say the sound of "**u**" in *rule*.

☐ I practiced my flashcards today. (Add the new cards.)

MORE ALPHABET REVIEW

As you write the letters across each line, say the sound of "**u**" in *put*.

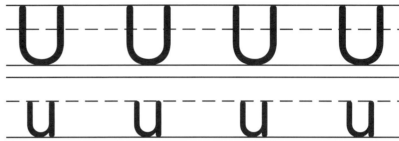

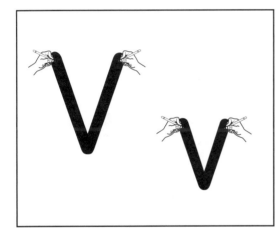

As you write the letters across each line, say the sound of "**w**" in *way*.

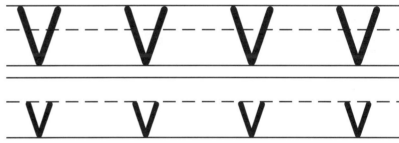

As you write the letters across each line, say the sound of "**ks**" in *socks*.

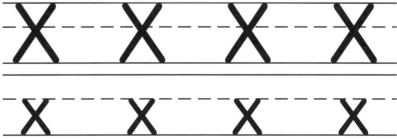

☐ I practiced my flashcards today. (Add the new cards.)

MORE ALPHABET REVIEW

As you write the letters across each line, form your lips to say **"oo"** but say **"ee"** instead. (Hold the sound longer than Latin y.)

Ȳ Ȳ Ȳ Ȳ

ȳ ȳ ȳ ȳ

As you write the letters across each line, form your lips to say **"oo"** but say **"ee"** instead. (Hold the sound shorter than Latin ȳ.)

Y Y Y Y

y y y y

As you write the letters across each line, say the sound of **"dz"** in *adze*.

Z Z Z Z

z z z z

☐ I practiced my flashcards today. (Add the new cards.)

LET'S PRACTICE

Match the letters with their sounds.

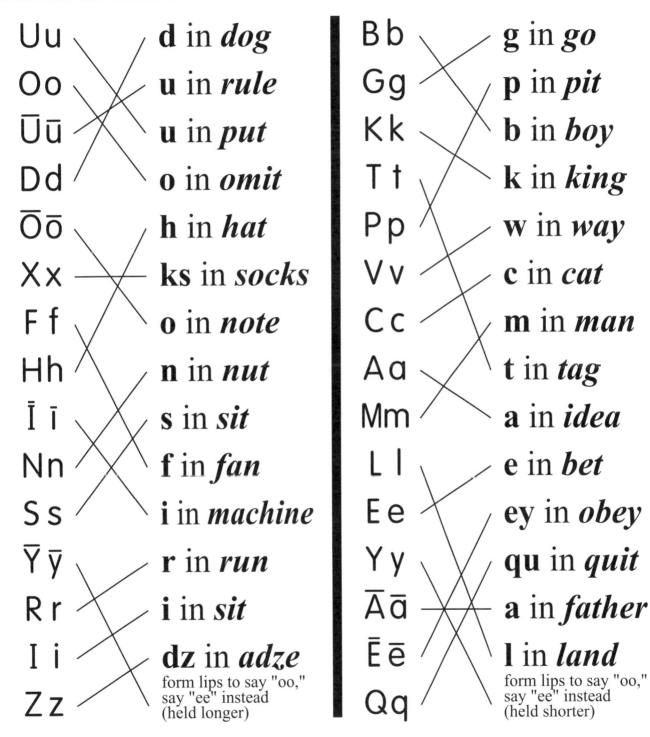

☐ I practiced my flashcards today.

LET'S REVIEW LATIN DIPHTHONGS

ae

As you write the diphthong **ae**, say the "*aye*" sound.

ae   ae   ae
ae   ae   ae

As you write the diphthong **au**, say the "**ow**" sound in *now*.

au   au   au
au   au   au

au

ei

As you write the diphthong **ei**, say the "**ei**" sound in *neighbor*.

ei   ei   ei
ei   ei   ei

☐ I practiced my flashcards today. (Add the new cards.)

MORE LATIN DIPHTHONGS

As you write the diphthong eu, say "*ay-oo*" as one syllable.

eu	eu	eu
eu	eu	eu

eu

As you write the diphthong oe, say the "**oy**" sound in *joy*.

oe

oe	oe	oe
oe	oe	oe

As you write the diphthong ui, say the "**uee**" sound in *queen*.

ui	ui	ui
ui	ui	ui

ui

☐ I practiced my flashcards today. (Add the new cards.)

LET'S PRACTICE

Write the Latin letters for the sounds.

1. Latin **ui** sounds like **uee** in *queen*.

2. Latin **ei** sounds like **ei** in *neighbor*.

3. Latin **ae** sounds like *aye*.

4. Latin **eu** sounds like *ay-oo* (in one syllable).

5. Latin **au** sounds like **ow** in *now*.

6. Latin **oe** sounds like **oy** in *joy*.

☐ I practiced my flashcards today.

LET'S REVIEW SPECIAL CONSONANTS

As you write the consonants **bs**, say the "*ps*" sound.

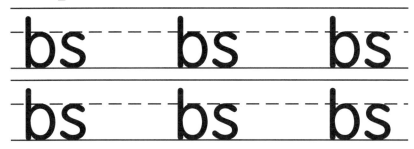

As you write the consonants **bt**, say the "*pt*" sound.

As you write the consonants **ch**, say the "**ch**" sound in *character*.

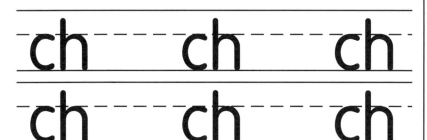

☐ I practiced my flashcards today. (Add the new cards.)

MORE SPECIAL CONSONANTS

As you write the consonants gu, say the "**gu**" sound in *anguish*.

As you write the consonant i, say the "**y**" sound in *youth*.

As you write the consonants ph, say the "**ph**" sound in *phone*.

☐ I practiced my flashcards today. (Add the new cards.)

MORE SPECIAL CONSONANTS

As you write the consonants **su**, say the "**su**" sound in *suave*.

su su su
su su su

su

th

As you write the consonants **th**, say the "**th**" sound in *thick*.

th th th
th th th

Write six Latin diphthongs.

ae au ei eu oe ui

Write eight Latin special consonants.

bs bt ch gu i ph su th

☐ I practiced my flashcards today. (Add the new cards.)

LET'S PRACTICE

Match the letters with their sounds.

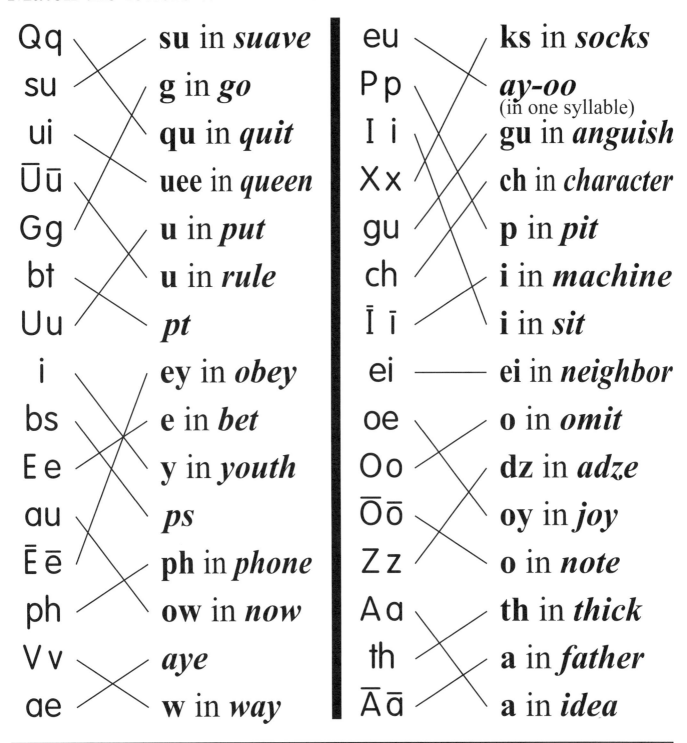

☐ I practiced my flashcards today.

LET'S PRACTICE

Circle the words with the Latin sounds.

ch	arch (car) child	**bt**	able (slept) debt	**th**	the this (throng)
g	gem age (good)	**ei**	diet (reign) seige	**v**	(wish) never vast
oe	(foil) poet toe	**au**	slow taught (cow)	**ō**	knob (vote) often
c	mice (can) race	**bs**	(hips) tabs ribs	**ī**	right hit (clean)
ui	(tweet) built suit	**su**	suit sun (swim)	**ē**	get (say) feet

☐ I practiced my flashcards today.

LET'S PRACTICE

Circle the correct Latin letters below the sounds.

u in *put*	th in *thick*	ey in *obey*
(Ūū) Uu	(th) t	(Ēē) Ee
a in *idea*	ow in *now*	i in *machine*
(Aa) Āā	(au) ae	I i (Ī ī)
uee in *queen*	i in *sit*	o in *note*
ue (ui)	Ī ī (I i)	(Ōō) Oo
u in *rule*	a in *father*	su in *suave*
(Ūū) Uu	(Āā) Aa	gu (su)
o in *omit*	e in *bet*	oy in *joy*
(Oo) Ōō	Ēē (Ee)	(oe) eu

☐ I practiced my flashcards today.

Lesson 5

puella

means

girl

Write the Latin word that means **girl**.

-------- puella --------

Circle the Latin words that mean **girl**.

puela   peula   peula
(puella)   pulla   pulla
peula   (puella)   peulla
peulla   pluea   (puella)

☐ I practiced my flashcards today. (Add the new card.)

LET'S PRACTICE

Fill in the missing letters on the Latin word that means **girl**.

pu_ell_a

Draw a line from the Latin word to its meaning.

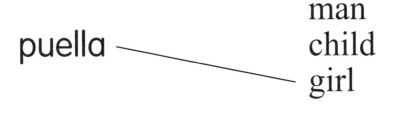

Draw a picture of a **puella**.

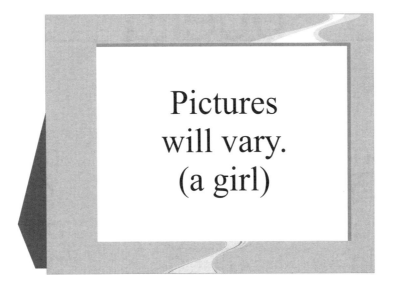

☐ I practiced my flashcards today.

vocō

means

I call

Write the Latin word that means **I call**.

vocō

Check the blank if the sentence is true.

_____ 1. vocō means **I want**.
_____ 2. puella means **child**.
___✓___ 3. vocō means **I call**.
___✓___ 4. puella means **girl**.

☐ I practiced my flashcards today. (Add the new card.)

LET'S PRACTICE

Circle the Latin words to match the meanings.

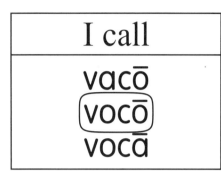
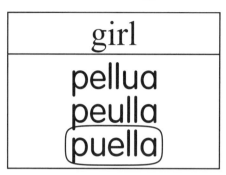

Unscramble the words and write them beside their meanings.

1. elpaul

2. coōv

I call vocō

girl puella

Write the meanings of the Latin words.

1. puella   girl

2. vocō   I call

☐ I practiced my flashcards today.

Lesson 6

puer

means

boy

Write the Latin word that means **boy**.

puer

Connect the words to the meanings in the ovals.

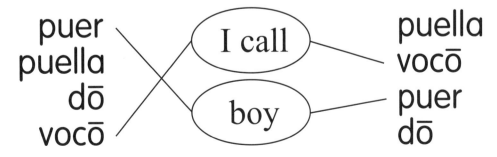

☐ I practiced my flashcards today. (Add the new card.)

LET'S PRACTICE

Fill in the missing letters. Then write what the words mean.

puer

It means __boy__

puella

It means __girl__

vocō

It means __I call__

Circle the Latin words to match the meanings.

I call	(vocō)	vacō
	voccō	voco

boy	pēur	peur
	pour	(puer)

girl	pullea	puela
	(puella)	pella

☐ I practiced my flashcards today.

dō

means

I give

Write the Latin word that means **I give**.

------------------ dō ------------------

Circle **yes** or **no**.

|yes| no   1. puer means **boy**.
yes |no| 2. dō means **I do**.
yes |no| 3. puella means **dress**.
|yes| no   4. vocō means **I call**.

☐ I practiced my flashcards today. (Add the new card.)

LET'S PRACTICE

Match the Latin words to their meanings.

<u> d </u> 1. puer   a. girl

<u> c </u> 2. vocō   b. I give

<u> b </u> 3. dō   c. I call

<u> a </u> 4. puella   d. boy

Write the meanings of the Latin words.

1. dō   <u>I give</u>

2. puer   <u>boy</u>

3. vocō   <u>I call</u>

4. puella   <u>girl</u>

☐ I practiced my flashcards today.

Lesson 7

agricola

means

farmer

Write the Latin word that means **farmer**.

------------------- agricola -------------------

Draw lines from the words to their meanings.

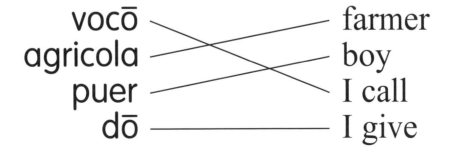

☐ I practiced my flashcards today. (Add the new card.)

Latin Workbook - Level 2
Copyright © 1997 by Karen Mohs

29

LET'S PRACTICE

Unscramble the words and write them beside their meanings.

1. eurp
2. lalupe
3. covō
4. ōd

I call **vocō**

I give **dō**

boy **puer**

girl **puella**

Circle the Latin words to match the meanings.

farmer		I give
vocō puer (agricola)		(dō) puella vocō

girl	I call	boy
(puella) puer agricola	agricola (vocō) puer	puella vocō (puer)

☐ I practiced my flashcards today.

aqua

means

water

Write the Latin word that means **water**.

aqua

Write the Latin words.

farmer agricola   I give dō

water aqua   boy puer

☐ I practiced my flashcards today. (Add the new card.)

LET'S PRACTICE

Fill in the blanks with the Latin words from the box.

aqua   agricola   dō

1. **dō** means **I give**.

2. **agricola** means **farmer**.

3. **aqua** means **water**.

Circle the meanings of the Latin words.

aqua		puella	
color	(water)	(girl)	boy

puer		vocō	
girl	(boy)	(I call)	I do

dō		agricola	
I call	(I give)	(farmer)	farm

☐ I practiced my flashcards today.

Lesson 8

est

means

he is, she is, it is, there is

Write the Latin word that means **he is**.

_____ est _____

Circle **yes** or **no**.

yes (no) 1. aqua means **blue**.
(yes) no 2. est means **she is**.
yes (no) 3. dō means **I make**.
(yes) no 4. agricola means **farmer**.

☐ I practiced my flashcards today. (Add the new card.)

LET'S PRACTICE

Write the meanings of the Latin words.

1. vocō — I call
2. puella — girl
3. dō — I give
4. aqua — water
5. puer — boy
6. est — he is, she is, it is, there is
7. agricola — farmer

Unscramble the words and write them beside their meanings.

1. aaqu
2. coōv
3. rupe
4. tes

- boy — puer
- water — aqua
- he is — est
- I call — vocō

☐ I practiced my flashcards today.

fēmina

means

woman

Write the Latin word that means **woman**.

fēmina

Circle the Latin words that mean **woman**.

(fēmina)   fīmena   fēnema
fēnima   feminā   (femīna)
femina   fēmana   (fēmina)
fāmina   (fēmina)   fēmena

☐ I practiced my flashcards today. (Add the new card.)

LET'S PRACTICE

Fill in the blanks with the Latin words from the box.

| puer | fēmina | est |

1. __est__ means **there is**.

2. __puer__ means **boy**.

3. __fēmina__ means **woman**.

Circle **yes** or **no**.

(yes) no 1. puella means **girl**.
yes (no) 2. agricola means **gold**.
(yes) no 3. fēmina means **woman**.
yes (no) 4. puer means **little**.
yes (no) 5. vocō means **win**.
(yes) no 6. est means **there is**.
(yes) no 7. aqua means **water**.
(yes) no 8. dō means **I give**.

☐ I practiced my flashcards today.

Lesson 9

et

means

and

Write the Latin word that means **and**.

et

Circle the Latin words to match the meanings.

woman	and	it is
(fēmina)	aqua	et
fortūna	(et)	(est)
filius	ad	sed

☐ I practiced my flashcards today. (Add the new card.)

LET'S PRACTICE

Circle the Latin words to match the meanings.

and	ete	(et)
	est	ēt

he is, she is, it is, there is	(est)	ēst
	ete	et

boy	puerre	peur
	(puer)	peurre

Write the Latin words.

woman __fēmina__   I give __dō__

I call __vocō__   girl __puella__

she is __est__   farmer __agricola__

water __aqua__   and __et__

☐ I practiced my flashcards today.

silva

means

forest

Write the Latin word that means **forest**.

silva

Fill in the missing letters. Then write what the words mean.

fēmina

It means woman

silva

It means forest

☐ I practiced my flashcards today. (Add the new card.)

LET'S PRACTICE

Match the Latin words to their meanings.

_i_	1. est	a.	woman
_h_	2. agricola	b.	water
_g_	3. puer	c.	forest
_e_	4. dō	d.	girl
_c_	5. silva	e.	I give
_f_	6. vocō	f.	I call
_d_	7. puella	g.	boy
_a_	8. fēmina	h.	farmer
_b_	9. aqua	i.	there is

Connect the words to the meanings in the ovals.

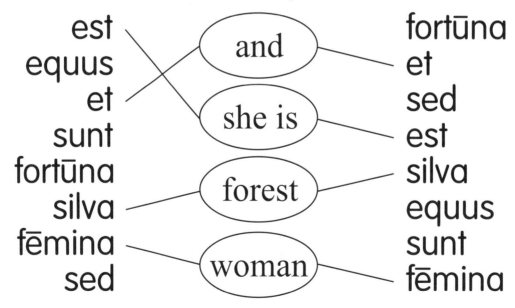

☐ I practiced my flashcards today.

LET'S REVIEW

Write the Latin letters for the sounds.

o in *note*	Ōō	i in *sit*	Ii
u in *rule*	Ūū	w in *way*	Vv
y in *youth*	i	oy in *joy*	oe
ks in *socks*	Xx	ey in *obey*	Ēē
pt	bt	u in *put*	Uu
n in *nut*	Nn	a in *idea*	Aa
e in *bet*	Ee	*aye*	ae
c in *cat*	Cc	a in *father*	Āā
o in *omit*	Oo	t in *tag*	Tt
ow in *now*	au	*ps*	bs

☐ I practiced my flashcards today.

LET'S PRACTICE

Draw a picture of a fēmina standing in a silva with a puer and a puella.

Pictures will vary.
(A woman is standing in a forest with a boy and a girl.)

☐ I practiced my flashcards today.

Lesson 11

īnsula

means

island

Write the Latin word that means **island**.

------- īnsula -------

Draw lines from the words to their meanings.

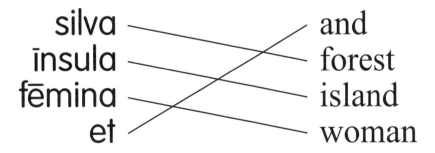

☐ I practiced my flashcards today. (Add the new card.)

LET'S PRACTICE

Check the blank if the sentence is true.

- ✓ 1. est means **it is**.
- ___ 2. puer means **fear**.
- ✓ 3. agricola means **farmer**.
- ✓ 4. īnsula means **island**.
- ___ 5. et means **I ate**.
- ✓ 6. fēmina means **woman**.
- ✓ 7. silva means **forest**.
- ___ 8. dō means **I do**.

Write the Latin words.

he is	est	boy	puer
forest	silva	water	aqua
girl	puella	I give	dō
island	īnsula	I call	vocō

☐ I practiced my flashcards today.

sunt

means

they are, there are

Write the Latin word that means **they are** or **there are**.

_____ sunt _____

Circle the Latin words to match the meanings.

there are	sent	sant
	sont	(sunt)
island	(īnsula)	īnsūla
	īnsala	īnsīla

☐ I practiced my flashcards today. (Add the new card.)

LET'S PRACTICE

Check the blank if the sentence is true.

_____	1. īnsula means **insult**.
✓	2. agricola means **farmer**.
_____	3. vocō means **crazy**.
_____	4. est means **we are**.
✓	5. puer means **boy**.
_____	6. aqua means **green**.
✓	7. sunt means **there are**.
✓	8. puella means **girl**.

Match the Latin words to their meanings.

_h_	1. est	a.	and
_c_	2. dō	b.	farmer
_g_	3. fēmina	c.	I give
_f_	4. īnsula	d.	boy
_b_	5. agricola	e.	forest
_a_	6. et	f.	island
_e_	7. silva	g.	woman
_i_	8. aqua	h.	there is
_d_	9. puer	i.	water

☐ I practiced my flashcards today.

Lesson 12

laudō

means

I praise

Write the Latin word that means **I praise**.

------------------ laudō ------------------

Circle the Latin words that mean **I praise**.

luadō	(laudō)	uladō
lāudo	laduō	leudō
aludō	laūdo	(laudō)
(laudō)	loudā	ladeō

☐ I practiced my flashcards today. (Add the new card.)

LET'S PRACTICE

Fill in the missing letters. Then write what the words mean.

īnsula

It means island

laudō

It means I praise

silva

It means forest

Write the meanings of the Latin words.

1. fēmina — woman
2. est — he is, she is, it is, there is
3. dō — I give
4. et — and
5. aqua — water
6. sunt — they are, there are
7. agricola — farmer

☐ I practiced my flashcards today.

nōn

means

not

Write the Latin word that means **not**.

_____ **nōn** _____

Circle the Latin words to match the meanings.

they are	not	I praise
sed	cum	(laudō)
(sunt)	amō	īnsula
silva	(nōn)	lingua

☐ I practiced my flashcards today. (Add the new card.)

LET'S PRACTICE

Draw lines from the words to their meanings.

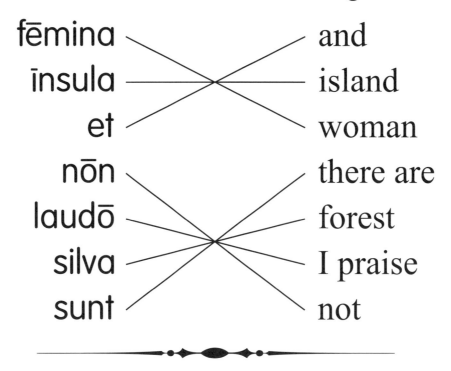

Unscramble the words and write them beside their meanings.

1. nuts
2. ōd
3. vails
4. aeullp

I give __dō__

girl __puella__

there are __sunt__

forest __silva__

☐ I practiced my flashcards today.

Lesson 13

ad

means

towards, to

Write the Latin word that means **towards** or **to**.

_____ **ad** _____

Fill in the blanks with the Latin words from the box.

nōn	ad

1. **ad** _____ means **towards**.
2. **nōn** _____ means **not**.

☐ I practiced my flashcards today. (Add the new card.)

LET'S PRACTICE

Circle **yes** or **no**.

- (yes) no 1. sunt means **there are**.
- (yes) no 2. et means **and**.
- (yes) no 3. īnsula means **island**.
- (yes) no 4. nōn means **not**.
- (yes) no 5. fēmina means **woman**.
- (yes) no 6. laudō means **I praise**.
- yes (no) 7. ad means **news**.
- yes (no) 8. silva means **coin**.

Circle the meanings of the Latin words.

vocō	
I sing	(I call)

agricola	
wheat	(farmer)

aqua	
(water)	green

puer	
(boy)	push

est	
she has	(she is)

dō	
I do	(I give)

☐ I practiced my flashcards today.

vīta

means

life

Write the Latin word that means **life**.

------------------ vīta ------------------

Connect the words to the meanings in the ovals.

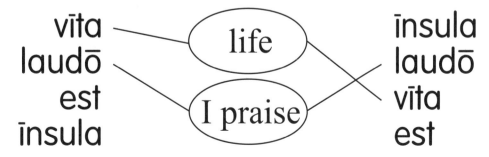

☐ I practiced my flashcards today. (Add the new card.)

LET'S PRACTICE

Write the Latin words.

Draw lines from the words to their meanings.

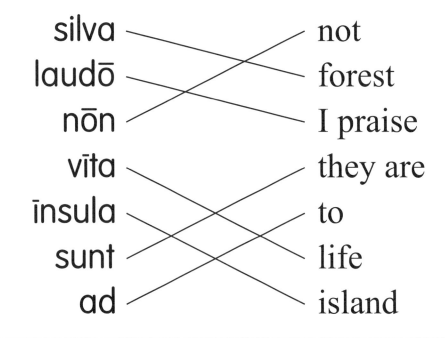

☐ I practiced my flashcards today.

Lesson 14

porta

means

gate

Write the Latin word that means **gate**.

------- **porta** -------

Write the meanings of the Latin words.

1. **silva**   forest
2. **porta**   gate
3. **vīta**   life
4. **īnsula**   island
5. **aqua**   water
6. **et**   and
7. **nōn**   not
8. **fēmina**   woman

☐ I practiced my flashcards today. (Add the new card.)

LET'S PRACTICE

Circle the Latin words to match the meanings.

and	not	island
est ad (et)	nauta (nōn) nātūra	prōvincia silva (īnsula)
forest	they are	life
(silva) patria terra	est (sunt) sed	laudō (vīta) vīlla

Fill in the missing letters. Then write what the words mean.

porta

It means __gate__

ad

It means __towards or to__

laudō

It means __I praise__

☐ I practiced my flashcards today.

memoria

means

memory

Write the Latin word that means **memory**.

memoria

Circle **yes** or **no**.

yes (no) 1. porta means **port**.
yes (no) 2. ad means **from**.
(yes) no 3. memoria means **memory**.
yes (no) 4. vīta means **vitamin**.

☐ I practiced my flashcards today. (Add the new card.)

LET'S PRACTICE

Unscramble the words and write them beside their meanings.

1. ste
2. stun
3. trapo
4. uslīna

island __īnsula__

it is __est__

there are __sunt__

gate __porta__

Circle the Latin words to match the meanings.

not	non	nunt
	(nōn)	nōne

memory	mēmoria	(memoria)
	memōria	momeria

life	vita	vitā
	vītta	(vīta)

☐ I practiced my flashcards today.

nāvigō

means

I sail

Write the Latin word that means **I sail**.

nāvigō

Circle the Latin words that mean **I sail**.

nāvigo	nivāgō	navigō
nēvagō	novegō	(nāvigō)
(nāvigō)	navīgō	nōvigā
nāvōgi	(nāvigō)	nāvīgō

☐ I practiced my flashcards today. (Add the new card.)

LET'S PRACTICE

Connect the words to the meanings in the ovals.

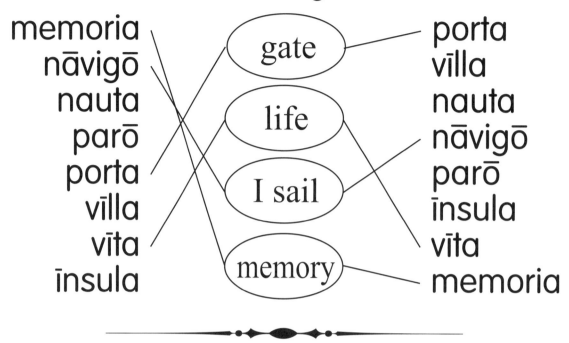

Fill in the blanks with the Latin words from the box.

| nōn | laudō | ad |

1. __ad__ means **to**.

2. __laudō__ means **I praise**.

3. __nōn__ means **not**.

☐ I practiced my flashcards today.

sed

means

but

Write the Latin word that means **but**.

———————————— sed ————————————

Match the Latin words to their meanings.

  _d_   1. memoria   a. but
  _c_   2. porta   b. I sail
  _a_   3. sed   c. gate
  _b_   4. nāvigō   d. memory

☐ I practiced my flashcards today. (Add the new card.)

LET'S PRACTICE

Circle the meanings of the Latin words.

fēmina		et	
(woman)	fame	eat	(and)

est		īnsula	
east	(it is)	warm	(island)

sunt		silva	
stamp	(they are)	(forest)	metal

Check the blank if the sentence is true.

✓ 1. sed means **but**.
___ 2. nōn means **none**.
✓ 3. laudō means **I praise**.
✓ 4. ad means **towards**.
✓ 5. vīta means **life**.
___ 6. porta means **suitcase**.
___ 7. memoria means **money**.
___ 8. nāvigō means **I push**.

☐ I practiced my flashcards today.

LET'S PRACTICE

Color the hourglass green if the words mean the same.

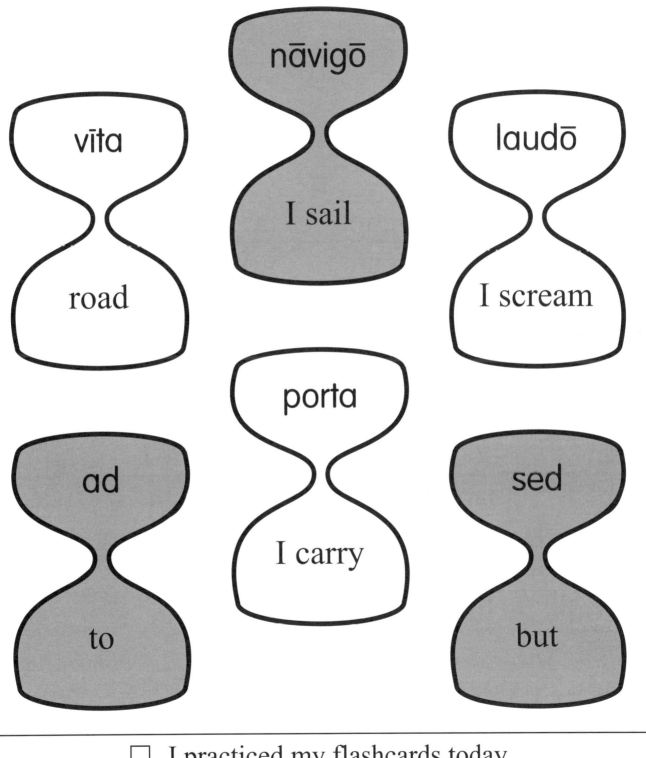

☐ I practiced my flashcards today.

LET'S PRACTICE

Circle the words that have the sounds of the Latin letters.

eat (west) **e** (get) tea	(good) (gas) **g** age gym	twine build **ui** (weed) (sweet)
only (flower) **au** low (sour)	greet see **ē** (vane) (say)	chair (arc) **ch** (chasm) chin
(hops) tabs **bs** (sips) absent	(bean) grin **ī** been (green)	fun purr **ū** (tool) (mood)
(put) (book) **u** hut boot	(swing) suit **su** (swim) sure	(firm) oven **f** vast (after)
(able) (back) **b** pan lips	(boat) (hope) **ō** some hook	van (wash) **v** valley (away)
(broil) (toy) **oe** toe poem	cent (acre) **c** (care) arch	ride sign **i** (dip) (spin)

☐ I practiced my flashcards today.

Lesson 17

fortūna

means

fortune, chance

Write the Latin word that means **fortune** or **chance**.

fortūna

Circle the Latin words that mean **fortune** or **chance**.

fartūna　　　　fūrtona　　　　(fortūna)
fortuna　　　　fōrtona　　　　furtāna
fōrtuna　　　　fotrūna　　　　fōrtūnā
(fortūna)　　　(fortūna)　　　fornūta

☐ I practiced my flashcards today. (Add the new card.)

LET'S PRACTICE

Fill in the blanks with the Latin words from the box.

| nōn | vīta | ad |

1. **vīta** means **life**.

2. **nōn** means **not**.

3. **ad** means **towards**.

Circle the Latin words to match the meanings.

life	I sail	chance
(vīta)	nātūra	fīlius
vīlla	(nāvigō)	fēmina
via	nauta	(fortūna)

but	memory	gate
silva	littera	(porta)
sunt	(memoria)	portō
(sed)	lingua	parō

☐ I practiced my flashcards today.

via

means

road, way

Write the Latin word that means **road** or **way**.

via

Draw lines from the words to their meanings.

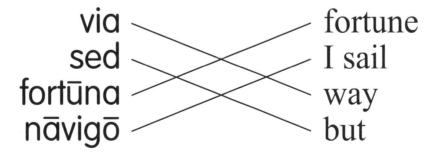

☐ I practiced my flashcards today. (Add the new card.)

LET'S PRACTICE

Write the meanings of the Latin words.

1. memoria — memory
2. porta — gate
3. vīta — life
4. sed — but
5. nāvigō — I sail
6. via — road or way
7. fortūna — fortune or chance

Unscramble the words and write them beside their meanings.

1. ōnn | towards — ad
2. aēinmf | not — nōn
3. da | I praise — laudō
4. aōudl | woman — fēmina

☐ I practiced my flashcards today.

Lesson 18

portō

means

I carry

Write the Latin word that means **I carry**.

portō

Circle the meanings of the Latin words.

nāvigō	
sailor	(I sail)

portō	
(I carry)	gate

fortūna	
treasure	(chance)

via	
life	(road)

☐ I practiced my flashcards today. (Add the new card.)

LET'S PRACTICE

Circle **yes** or **no**.

- yes [no] 1. memoria means **album**.
- [yes] no 2. nāvigō means **I sail**.
- yes [no] 3. porta means **I carry**.
- yes [no] 4. fortūna means **bank**.
- [yes] no 5. vīta means **life**.
- [yes] no 6. via means **way**.
- yes [no] 7. portō means **gate**.
- [yes] no 8. sed means **but**.

Write the Latin words.

- forest **silva**
- towards **ad**
- island **īnsula**
- and **et**
- not **nōn**
- I praise **laudō**
- water **aqua**
- they are **sunt**

☐ I practiced my flashcards today.

quid

means

what
(a question)

Write the Latin word that means **what** (a question).

------------------- quid -------------------

Circle the Latin words to match the meanings.

what?	(quid)	quide
	qued	guid
I carry	partō	purtō
	portā	(portō)

☐ I practiced my flashcards today. (Add the new card.)

LET'S PRACTICE

Match the Latin words to their meanings.

<u> e </u> 1. nāvigō   a. towards
<u> f </u> 2. memoria   b. gate
<u> c </u> 3. sunt   c. there are
<u> g </u> 4. laudō   d. life
<u> b </u> 5. porta   e. I sail
<u> a </u> 6. ad   f. memory
<u> d </u> 7. vīta   g. I praise
<u> i </u> 8. sed   h. not
<u> h </u> 9. nōn   i. but

Connect the words to the meanings in the ovals.

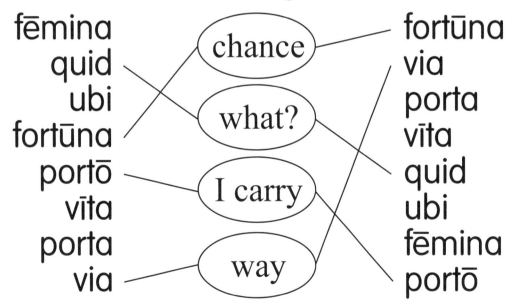

☐ I practiced my flashcards today.

Lesson 19

tuba

means

trumpet

Write the Latin word that means **trumpet**.

tuba

Fill in the missing letters. Then write what the words mean.

<u>t</u>ub<u>a</u>

It means trumpet

q<u>ui</u>d

It means what?

☐ I practiced my flashcards today. (Add the new card.)

LET'S PRACTICE

Check the blank if the sentence is true.

✓ 1. tuba means **trumpet**.
✓ 2. nāvigō means **I sail**.
✓ 3. fortūna means **chance**.
___ 4. sed means **I spoke**.
___ 5. portō means **I open**.
✓ 6. quid means **what?**
___ 7. via means **air**.
✓ 8. porta means **gate**.

Fill in the blanks with the Latin words from the box.

| puella | memoria | vīta |

1. **puella** means **girl**.

2. **memoria** means **memory**.

3. **vīta** means **life**.

☐ I practiced my flashcards today.

ager

means

field, territory

Write the Latin word that means **field** or **territory**.

ager

Write the meanings of the Latin words.

1. sed   but
2. via   road or way
3. nāvigō   I sail
4. fortūna   fortune or chance
5. quid   what?
6. ager   field or territory
7. tuba   trumpet
8. portō   I carry

☐ I practiced my flashcards today. (Add the new card.)

LET'S PRACTICE

Circle the Latin words to match the meanings.

towards	gate	not
et (**ad**) **dō**	(**porta**) poēta patria	nauta sed (**nōn**)

memory	I praise	life
nātūra prōvincia (**memoria**)	īnsula littera (**laudō**)	(**vīta**) ubi quid

---

Circle **yes** or **no**.

- yes (**no**) 1. **sed** means **word**.
- (**yes**) no 2. **nāvigō** means **I sail**.
- (**yes**) no 3. **tuba** means **trumpet**.
- yes (**no**) 4. **via** means **pill**.
- yes (**no**) 5. **portō** means **I eat**.
- yes (**no**) 6. **quid** means **slime**.
- (**yes**) no 7. **ager** means **territory**.
- yes (**no**) 8. **fortūna** means **chest**.

☐ I practiced my flashcards today.

Lesson 20

parō

means

I prepare, I prepare for

Write the Latin word that means **I prepare** or **I prepare for**.

parō

Unscramble the words and write them beside their meanings.

1. rōpa   territory   ager

2. rage   I prepare   parō

☐ I practiced my flashcards today. (Add the new card.)

LET'S PRACTICE

Circle the meanings of the Latin words.

porta		nāvigō	
(gate)	dock	(I sail)	I guide

ad		memoria	
(to)	math	album	(memory)

vīta		sed	
grow	(life)	(but)	seed

Draw lines from the words to their meanings.

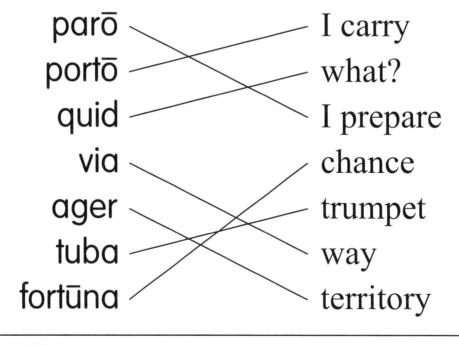

parō — I prepare
portō — I carry
quid — what?
via — way
ager — territory
tuba — trumpet
fortūna — chance

☐ I practiced my flashcards today.

amīcus

means

friend

Write the Latin word that means **friend**.

amīcus

Fill in the blanks with the Latin words from the box.

| parō | amīcus |

1. **parō** means **I prepare**.
2. **amīcus** means **friend**.

☐ I practiced my flashcards today. (Add the new card.)

LET'S PRACTICE

Write the Latin words.

I prepare **parō**   chance **fortūna**

but **sed**   friend **amīcus**

trumpet **tuba**   I carry **portō**

I sail **nāvigō**   memory **memoria**

Circle the Latin words to match the meanings.

road way	vīa	(vīa)
	vea	vēa

field territory	agger	aeger
	(ager)	āger

what?	(quid)	qiud
	qeud	qued

☐ I practiced my flashcards today.

Lesson 21

spectō

means

I look at

Write the Latin word that means **I look at**.

spectō

Circle **yes** or **no**.

(yes) no   1. ager means **field**.
(yes) no   2. spectō means **I look at**.
yes (no)   3. parō means **I eat**.
yes (no)   4. amīcus means **minus**.

☐ I practiced my flashcards today. (Add the new card.)

LET'S PRACTICE

Connect the words to the meanings in the ovals.

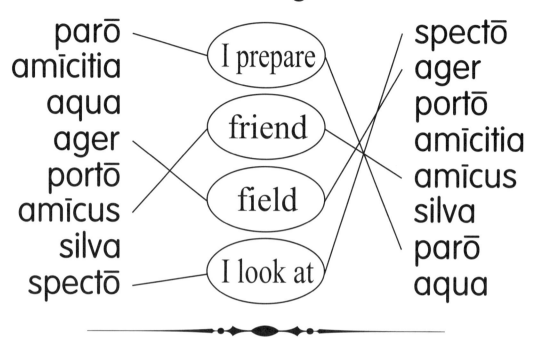

Check the blank if the sentence is true.

_____	1. parō means **I cut**.
✓	2. fortūna means **chance**.
_____	3. ager means **mad**.
✓	4. via means **road**.
_____	5. spectō means **I wash**.
✓	6. portō means **I carry**.
_____	7. tuba means **straw**.
_____	8. quid means **fish**.
✓	9. sed means **but**.

☐ I practiced my flashcards today.

nātūra

means

nature

Write the Latin word that means **nature**.

------- **nātūra** -------

Match the Latin words to their meanings.

<u>c</u> 1. parō   a. nature
<u>d</u> 2. spectō   b. friend
<u>b</u> 3. amīcus   c. I prepare for
<u>a</u> 4. nātūra   d. I look at

☐ I practiced my flashcards today. (Add the new card.)

LET'S PRACTICE

Fill in the missing letters. Then write what the words mean.

nātūra

It means __nature__

ager

It means __field or territory__

amīcus

It means __friend__

Circle the meanings of the Latin words.

portō		specto	
(I carry)	I drink	I study	(I look at)

tuba		via	
pipe	(trumpet)	life	(road)

parō		quid	
I peel	(I prepare)	(what?)	who?

☐ I practiced my flashcards today.

LET'S PRACTICE

Connect the bubbles to the bubble pipes.

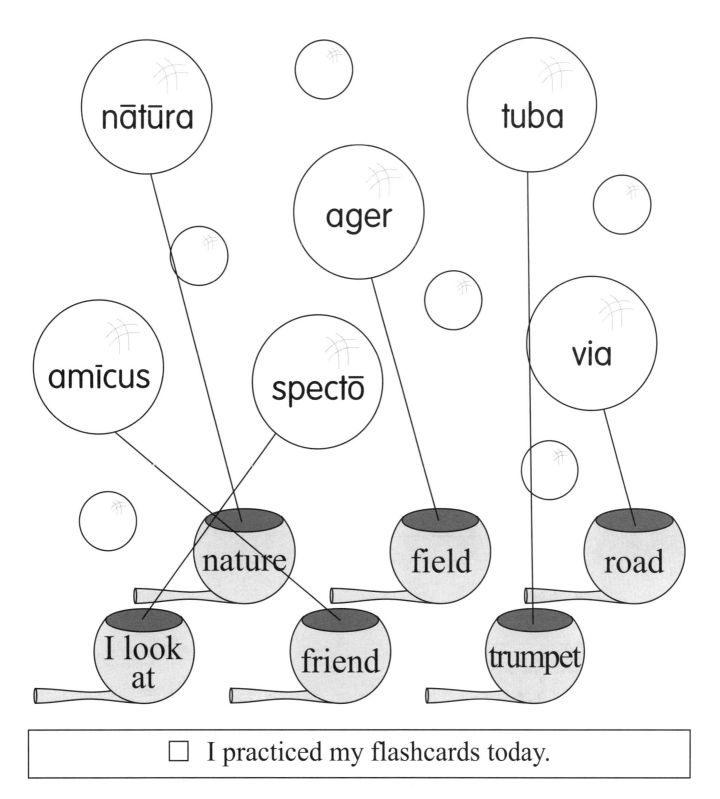

☐ I practiced my flashcards today.

PUZZLE TIME

Circle five Latin words. Write them below.

f	v	l	a	u	d	ō
g	i	t	d	p	ō	p
p	a	r	ō	k	c	i
s	m	p	ē	n	h	d

1. **laudō** means **I praise**.

2. **parō** means **I prepare**.

3. **via** means **way**.

4. **ad** means **toward**.

5. **dō** means **I give**.

☐ I practiced my flashcards today.

Lesson 23

campus

means

field, plain

Write the Latin word that means **field** or **plain**.

campus

Circle the Latin words to match the meanings.

I look at	nature	field
silva	porta	gladius
pugnō	(nātūra)	cum
(spectō)	nauta	(campus)

☐ I practiced my flashcards today. (Add the new card.)

LET'S PRACTICE

Fill in the blanks with the Latin words from the box.

via	portō	quid

1. **via** means **road**.
2. **quid** means **what?**
3. **portō** means **I carry**.

Write the meanings of the Latin words.

1. nātūra — nature
2. campus — field or plain
3. spectō — I look at
4. amīcus — friend
5. tuba — trumpet
6. ager — field or territory
7. parō — I prepare or I prepare for

☐ I practiced my flashcards today.

occupō

means

I seize, I capture

Write the Latin word that means **I seize** or **I capture**.

occupō

Circle the Latin words that mean **I seize** or **I capture**.

(occupō)	ācupō	(occupō)
ocupō	(occupō)	ōccupō
occūpō	ocuppō	occūpo
ocoupō	occapō	accupō

☐ I practiced my flashcards today. (Add the new card.)

LET'S PRACTICE

Unscramble the words and write them beside their meanings.

1. aiv   life **vīta**
2. iuqd   I carry **portō**
3. rōtop   road **via**
4. taīv   what? **quid**

Circle **yes** or **no**.

(yes)	no	1. spectō means **I look at**.
(yes)	no	2. parō means **I prepare for**.
(yes)	no	3. amīcus means **friend**.
(yes)	no	4. ager means **field**.
yes	**(no)**	5. occupō means **I sleep**.
yes	**(no)**	6. nātūra means **nation**.
yes	**(no)**	7. tuba means **bathtub**.
yes	**(no)**	8. campus means **tent**.

☐ I practiced my flashcards today.

Lesson 24

cum

means

with

Write the Latin word that means **with**.

cum

Write the Latin words.

I seize occupō   nature nātūra

plain campus   with cum

☐ I practiced my flashcards today. (Add the new card.)

Latin Workbook - Level 2
Copyright © 1997 by Karen Mohs

LET'S PRACTICE

Draw lines from the words to their meanings.

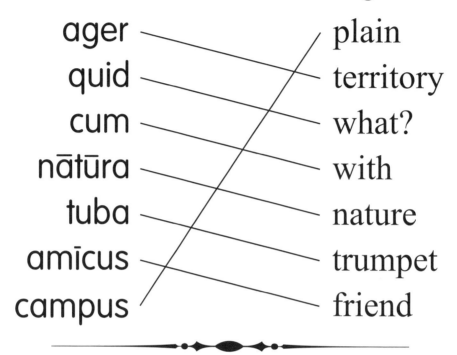

Fill in the missing letters. Then write what the words mean.

spectō

It means I look at

occupō

It means I seize or I capture

parō

It means I prepare or I prepare for

☐ I practiced my flashcards today.

nauta

means

sailor

Write the Latin word that means **sailor**.

------------------------------ nauta ------------------------------

Connect the words to the meanings in the ovals.

nauta   (field)   campus
amīcus   nātūra
nātūra   amīcus
campus   (sailor)   nauta

☐ I practiced my flashcards today. (Add the new card.)

LET'S PRACTICE

Circle the Latin words to match the meanings.

friend	ammīcus	amīccus
	(amīcus)	amīecus

sailor	neuta	(nauta)
	natua	nueta

I look at	speccō	spertō
	spettō	(spectō)

Match the Latin words to their meanings.

- _f_ 1. quid
- _g_ 2. nātūra
- _h_ 3. portō
- _c_ 4. parō
- _a_ 5. occupō
- _e_ 6. tuba
- _d_ 7. ager
- _i_ 8. cum
- _b_ 9. campus

a. I capture
b. plain
c. I prepare for
d. territory
e. trumpet
f. what?
g. nature
h. I carry
i. with

☐ I practiced my flashcards today.

Lesson 25

vīlla

means

farmhouse

Write the Latin word that means **farmhouse**.

vīlla

Check the blank if the sentence is true.

✓   1. nātūra means **nature**.
___   2. spectō means **I expect**.
✓   3. cum means **with**.
___   4. vīlla means **village**.

☐ I practiced my flashcards today. (Add the new card.)

LET'S PRACTICE

Write the meanings of the Latin words.

1. nātūra — nature
2. ager — field or territory
3. parō — I prepare or I prepare for
4. spectō — I look at
5. nauta — sailor
6. amīcus — friend
7. occupō — I seize or I capture

Fill in the missing letters. Then write what the words mean.

vīlla
It means farmhouse

campus
It means field or plain

cum
It means with

☐ I practiced my flashcards today.

littera

means

letter

Write the Latin word that means **letter**.

littera

Circle the Latin words that mean **letter**.

literra   lettira   letera
līttira   lattira   (littera)
(littera)   (littera)   litterā
littēra   lēttera   lāttera

☐ I practiced my flashcards today. (Add the new card.)

LET'S PRACTICE

Circle **yes** or **no**.

(yes) no   1. nauta means **sailor**.
(yes) no   2. littera means **letter**.
yes (no)   3. vīlla means **wish**.
yes (no)   4. occupō means **work**.
(yes) no   5. nātūra means **nature**.
(yes) no   6. campus means **plain**.
yes (no)   7. spectō means **careful**.
yes (no)   8. cum means **arrive**.

Match the Latin words to their meanings.

 b 1. fortūna   a. I prepare
 h 2. amīcus   b. chance
 g 3. ad   c. life
 f 4. via   d. trumpet
 a 5. parō   e. gate
 c 6. vīta   f. way
 i 7. sed   g. towards
 d 8. tuba   h. friend
 e 9. porta   i. but

☐ I practiced my flashcards today.

Lesson 26

ubi

means

where
(a question)

Write the Latin word that means **where** (a question).

ubi

Draw lines from the words to their meanings.

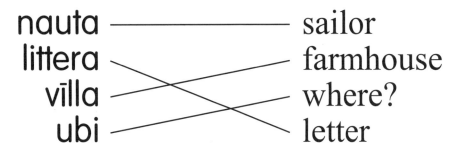

☐ I practiced my flashcards today. (Add the new card.)

LET'S PRACTICE

Circle the Latin words to match the meanings.

farmhouse	with	where?
prōvincia via **(vīlla)**	nōn **(cum)** quid	ager **(ubi)** tuba

I capture	sailor	letter
(occupō) portō laudō	**(nauta)** puer nāvigō	spectō **(littera)** lingua

---

Write the Latin words.

what? **quid**　　friend **amīcus**

I look at **spectō**　　plain **campus**

territory **ager**　　trumpet **tuba**

I prepare **parō**　　nature **nātūra**

☐ I practiced my flashcards today.

fīlius

means

son

Write the Latin word that means **son**.

fīlius

Circle the meanings of the Latin words.

vīlla	
(farmhouse)	village

fīlius	
file	(son)

littera	
litter	(letter)

nauta	
(sailor)	bad

☐ I practiced my flashcards today. (Add the new card.)

LET'S PRACTICE

Unscramble the words and write them beside their meanings.

1. scaīmu
2. cetsōp
3. ratānū
4. atbu

nature __nātūra__

I look at __spectō__

trumpet __tuba__

friend __amīcus__

Circle the Latin words to match the meanings.

I seize I capture	occūpo	ocupō
	ocuppō	(occupō)

sailor	(nauta)	naūta
	nautā	nuata

son	filēus	filīus
	(filius)	filuis

☐ I practiced my flashcards today.

Lesson 27

patria

means

country, native land

Write the Latin word that means **country** or **native land**.

------- patria -------

Connect the words to the meanings in the ovals.

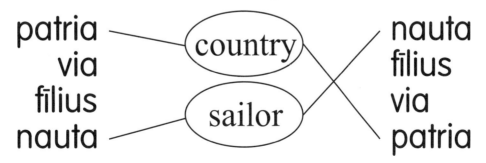

☐ I practiced my flashcards today. (Add the new card.)

LET'S PRACTICE

Check the blank if the sentence is true.

_____ 1. occupō means **I sit**.
_____ 2. ubi means **why?**
✓ 3. nauta means **sailor**.
✓ 4. fīlius means **son**.
✓ 5. littera means **letter**.
✓ 6. cum means **with**.
✓ 7. vīlla means **farmhouse**.
_____ 8. campus means **camp**.

Fill in the blanks with the Latin words from the box.

| nātūra | spectō | patria |

1. **patria** means **country**.
2. **nātūra** means **nature**.
3. **spectō** means **I look at**.

☐ I practiced my flashcards today.

fīlia

means

daughter

Write the Latin word that means **daughter**.

fīlia

Circle the Latin words to match the meanings.

daughter	where?	country
(fīlia)	(ubi)	prōvincia
fēmina	via	porta
fīlius	quid	(patria)

☐ I practiced my flashcards today. (Add the new card.)

LET'S PRACTICE

Fill in the missing letters. Then write what the words mean.

fīlia

It means daughter

littera

It means letter

fīlius

It means son

Write the meanings of the Latin words.

1. cum   with
2. occupō   I seize or I capture
3. ubi   where?
4. campus   field or plain
5. vīlla   farmhouse
6. patria   country or native land
7. nauta   sailor

☐ I practiced my flashcards today.

Lesson 28

LET'S PRACTICE

Draw a picture of an **amīcus** in an **ager** looking **ad** a **vīlla**.

Pictures will vary.
(A friend is in a field looking toward a farmhouse.)

☐ I practiced my flashcards today.

PUZZLE TIME

Circle five Latin words. Write them below.

v	ī	l	l	a	z	a
i	ȳ	ā	s	g	ū	q
a	m	h	ī	e	x	u
c	p	a	t	r	i	a

1. **vīlla** means **farmhouse**.

2. **patria** means **native land**.

3. **via** means **road**.

4. **ager** means **territory**.

5. **aqua** means **water**.

☐ I practiced my flashcards today.

Lesson 29

amīcitia

means

friendship

Write the Latin word that means **friendship**.

amīcitia

Circle the Latin words that mean **friendship**.

(amīcitia)   amīcitia   amīticia
amicitia   amīcītia   amīcītia
acīmitia   (amīcitia) (amīcitia)
āmīcitia   āmīcitia   amīcitai

☐ I practiced my flashcards today. (Add the new card.)

LET'S PRACTICE

Draw lines from the words to their meanings.

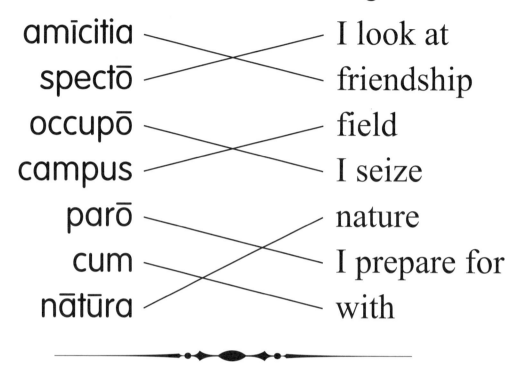

Circle **yes** or **no**.

yes	(no)	1. nauta means **nature**.
(yes)	no	2. vīlla means **farmhouse**.
(yes)	no	3. amīcus means **friend**.
yes	(no)	4. fīlia means **pony**.
yes	(no)	5. patria means **I clap**.
(yes)	no	6. ubi means **where?**
yes	(no)	7. littera means **clutter**.
(yes)	no	8. fīlius means **son**.

☐ I practiced my flashcards today.

amō

means

I love, I like

Write the Latin word that means **I love** or **I like**.

amō

Write the Latin words.

where? ubi   son fīlius

I love amō   letter littera

☐ I practiced my flashcards today. (Add the new card.)

LET'S PRACTICE

Circle the Latin words to match the meanings.

with	(cum)	cōm
	cūm	com

friendship	amīcittia	amīccitia
	(amīcitia)	ammīcitia

farmhouse	vīlia	vīllia
	vīla	(vīlla)

Unscramble the words and write them beside their meanings.

1. pōocuc   I love   **amō**

2. ōam   where?   **ubi**

3. aīlvl   I seize   **occupō**

4. ibu   farmhouse   **vīlla**

☐ I practiced my flashcards today.

Lesson 30

lingua

means

tongue, language

Write the Latin word that means **tongue** or **language**.

_____ **lingua** _____

Fill in the blanks with the Latin words from the box.

amō	lingua

1. __**lingua**__ means **language**.

2. __**amō**__ means **I like**.

☐ I practiced my flashcards today. (Add the new card.)

LET'S PRACTICE

Circle the meanings of the Latin words.

amīcitia	
show	(friendship)

puer	
(boy)	son

lingua	
line	(tongue)

amō	
(I like)	bullet

vīlla	
(farmhouse)	valley

vocō	
word	(I call)

Match the Latin words to their meanings.

- e 1. patria
- h 2. filia
- f 3. occupō
- g 4. littera
- i 5. cum
- d 6. ubi
- b 7. nauta
- a 8. campus
- c 9. filius

- a. field
- b. sailor
- c. son
- d. where?
- e. native land
- f. I seize
- g. letter
- h. daughter
- i. with

☐ I practiced my flashcards today.

equus

means

horse

Write the Latin word that means **horse**.

equus

Check the blank if the sentence is true.

_____	1. amīcitia means **happiness**.
✓	2. equus means **horse**.
✓	3. lingua means **language**.
_____	4. amō means **I am**.

☐ I practiced my flashcards today. (Add the new card.)

LET'S PRACTICE

Connect the words to the meanings in the ovals.

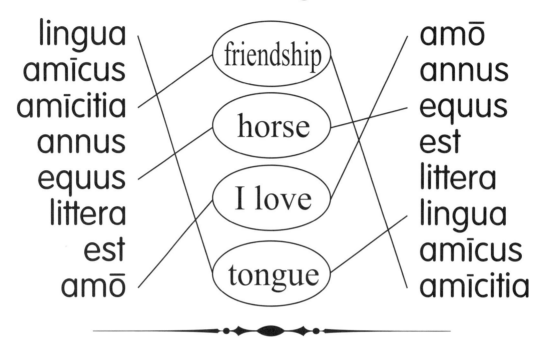

Circle the meanings of the Latin words.

patria	
father	(country)

littera	
(letter)	trash

ubi	
(where?)	which?

fīlius	
boy	(son)

fīlia	
(daughter)	girl

vīlla	
(farmhouse)	village

☐ I practiced my flashcards today.

Lesson 31

poēta

means

poet

Write the Latin word that means **poet**.

<u>   poēta   </u>

Fill in the missing letters. Then write what the words mean.

equus
It means <u>horse</u>

poēta
It means <u>poet</u>

☐ I practiced my flashcards today. (Add the new card.)

LET'S PRACTICE

Unscramble the words and write them beside their meanings.

1. ingōāv   sailor   __nauta__
2. tunaa   I sail   __nāvigō__
3. rimomea   farmer   __agricola__
4. liacgroa   memory   __memoria__

Draw lines from the words to their meanings.

- equus — horse
- amīcitia — friendship
- lingua — language
- patria — native land
- poēta — poet
- amō — I like
- fīlia — daughter

☐ I practiced my flashcards today.

annus

means

year

Write the Latin word that means **year**.

annus

Write the meanings of the Latin words.

1. fīlius — son
2. poēta — poet
3. vīlla — farmhouse
4. fīlia — daughter
5. ubi — where?
6. littera — letter
7. equus — horse
8. annus — year

☐ I practiced my flashcards today. (Add the new card.)

LET'S PRACTICE

Write the Latin words.

son	fīlius	I like	amō
country	patria	daughter	fīlia
where?	ubi	letter	littera
farmhouse	vīlla	friend	amīcus

Connect the words to the meanings in the ovals.

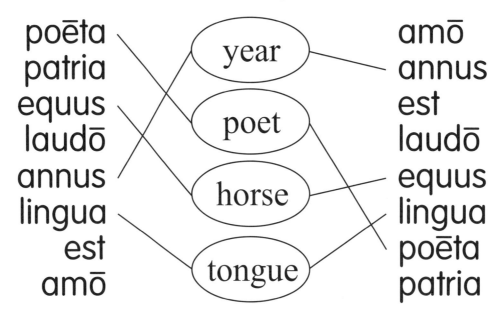

☐ I practiced my flashcards today.

Lesson 32

pugnō

means

I fight

Write the Latin word that means **I fight**.

pugnō

Circle yes or no.

(yes) no   1. annus means **year**.
yes (no)   2. poēta means **I write**.
yes (no)   3. pugnō means **I pick**.
(yes) no   4. equus means **horse**.

☐ I practiced my flashcards today. (Add the new card.)

LET'S PRACTICE

Fill in the blanks with the Latin words from the box.

| patria | amīcitia | fīlia |

1. **amīcitia** means **friendship**.

2. **fīlia** means **daughter**.

3. **patria** means **native land**.

Circle the Latin words to match the meanings.

I love	I fight	language
(amō)	puella	littera
amīcitia	(pugnō)	laudō
amīcus	puer	(lingua)

year	poet	horse
aqua	parō	est
ager	(poēta)	(equus)
(annus)	porta	et

☐ I practiced my flashcards today.

terra

means

earth, land

Write the Latin word that means **earth** or **land**.

terra

Circle the Latin words to match the meanings.

I fight	pognē	pagnā
	(pugnō)	pagnō
earth	teara	tera
	(terra)	tirra

☐ I practiced my flashcards today. (Add the new card.)

LET'S PRACTICE

Match the Latin words to their meanings.

_f_	1. littera	a.	farmhouse
_c_	2. annus	b.	where?
_e_	3. patria	c.	year
_a_	4. vīlla	d.	I capture
_d_	5. occupō	e.	country
_h_	6. filius	f.	letter
_i_	7. nauta	g.	with
_b_	8. ubi	h.	son
_g_	9. cum	i.	sailor

Check the blank if the sentence is true.

- ✓ 1. poēta means **poet**.
- ✓ 2. pugnō means **I fight**.
- ___ 3. amō means **I fire**.
- ✓ 4. amīcitia means **friendship**.
- ✓ 5. equus means **horse**.
- ___ 6. filia means **son**.
- ___ 7. lingua means **noodle**.
- ✓ 8. terra means **land**.

☐ I practiced my flashcards today.

Lesson 33

gladius

means

sword

Write the Latin word that means **sword**.

gladius

Circle the Latin words that mean **sword**.

glādius	glādīus	gildaus
galdius	gladuis	(gladius)
gladīus	(gladius)	glādīūs
(gladius)	gladiūs	glidaus

☐ I practiced my flashcards today. (Add the new card.)

LET'S PRACTICE

Circle the Latin words to match the meanings.

I fight	poet	earth
laudō specto **(pugnō)**	puella **(poēta)** porta	patria **(terra)** agricola

sword	year	horse
(gladius) puer fortūna	**(annus)** fīlius ad	campus **(equus)** amīcus

Fill in the blanks with the Latin words from the box.

| amīcitia | amō | lingua |

1. **amō** means **I love**.

2. **lingua** means **tongue**.

3. **amīcitia** means **friendship**.

☐ I practiced my flashcards today.

prōvincia

means

province

Write the Latin word that means **province**.

prōvincia

Draw lines from the words to their meanings.

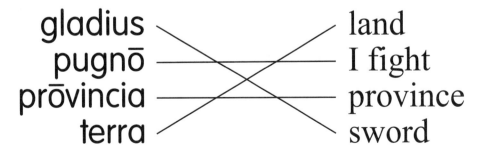

☐ I practiced my flashcards today. (Add the new card.)

LET'S PRACTICE

Write the meanings of the Latin words.

1. poēta   _poet_
2. annus   _year_
3. prōvincia   _province_
4. terra   _earth or land_
5. pugnō   _I fight_
6. gladius   _sword_
7. equus   _horse_

Unscramble the words and write them beside their meanings.

1. aaiprt   plain   **campus**
2. mcu   language   **lingua**
3. aucsmp   country   **patria**
4. aiugnl   with   **cum**

☐ I practiced my flashcards today.

Lesson 34

LET'S PRACTICE

Write the Latin words.

plain **campus**   country **patria**

friend **amīcus**   with **cum**

girl **puella**   son **fīlius**

daughter **fīlia**   I like **amō**

Circle **yes** or **no**.

yes (no)   1. pugnō means **I stop**.
yes (no)   2. lingua means **debate**.
(yes) no   3. prōvincia means **province**.
(yes) no   4. annus means **year**.
(yes) no   5. equus means **horse**.
(yes) no   6. poēta means **poet**.
yes (no)   7. gladius means **gift**.
yes (no)   8. terra means **plant**.

☐ I practiced my flashcards today.

LET'S PRACTICE

Match the Latin words to their meanings.

<u> i </u> 1. fīlia   a. I fight
<u> e </u> 2. amīcus   b. boy
<u> g </u> 3. lingua   c. poet
<u> d </u> 4. terra   d. earth
<u> a </u> 5. pugnō   e. friend
<u> c </u> 6. poēta   f. sword
<u> h </u> 7. amō   g. tongue
<u> b </u> 8. puer   h. I like
<u> f </u> 9. gladius   i. daughter

Circle the Latin words to match the meanings.

year	annūs	unnas
	(annus)	anins

province	provincia	provinnia
	provēncia	**(prōvincia)**

horse	ēquus	**(equus)**
	eqqus	equis

☐ I practiced my flashcards today.

LET'S PRACTICE

Connect the words to the meanings in the ovals.

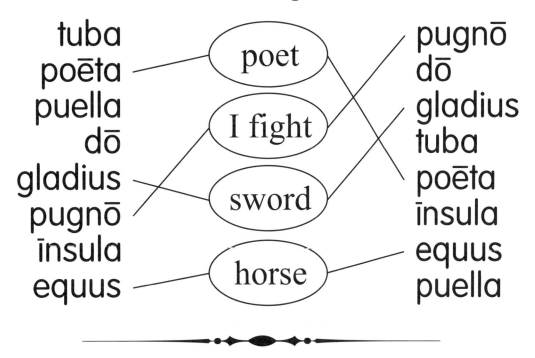

Fill in the missing letters. Then write what the words mean.

prōvincia

It means **province**

annus

It means **year**

terra

It means **earth or land**

☐ I practiced my flashcards today.

LET'S PRACTICE

Check the blank if the sentence is true.

✓	1. pugnō means **I fight**.
✓	2. annus means **year**.
✓	3. lingua means **tongue**.
___	4. equus means **add**.
___	5. terra means **afraid**.
___	6. prōvincia means **shout**.
___	7. gladius means **happy**.
✓	8. amō means **I like**.

Circle the meanings of the Latin words.

fīlia		ubi	
(daughter)	colt	why?	(where?)

fīlius		amīcus	
(son)	file	(friend)	less

poēta		patria	
manner	(poet)	(country)	flower

☐ I practiced my flashcards today.

LET'S PRACTICE

Write the Latin words on the chimneys.

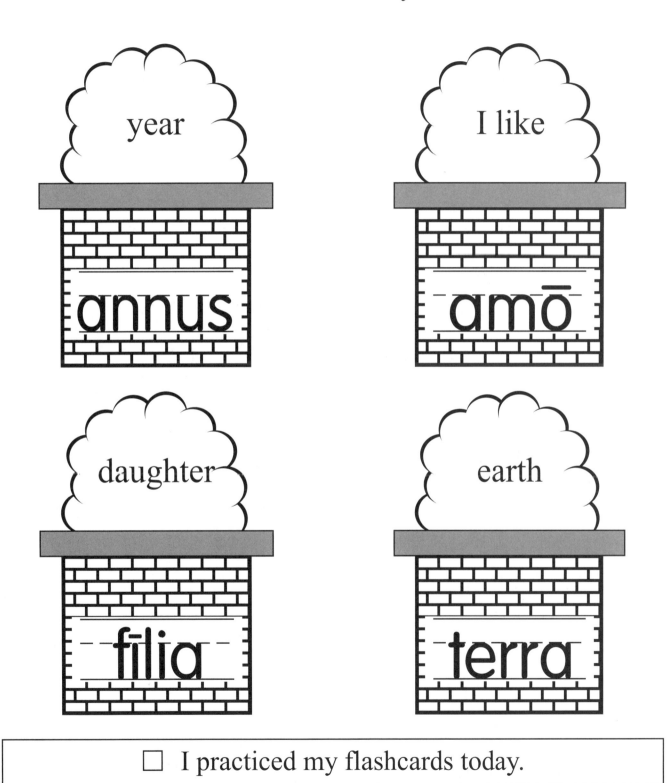

☐ I practiced my flashcards today.

PUZZLE TIME

Think of the meanings of the English words. Then write the Latin words on the puzzle below.

across
1. friendship
2. province
7. I give
9. I sail
11. plain
12. I prepare for

down
1. I love
3. I call
4. sailor
5. not
6. I carry
8. life
10. way

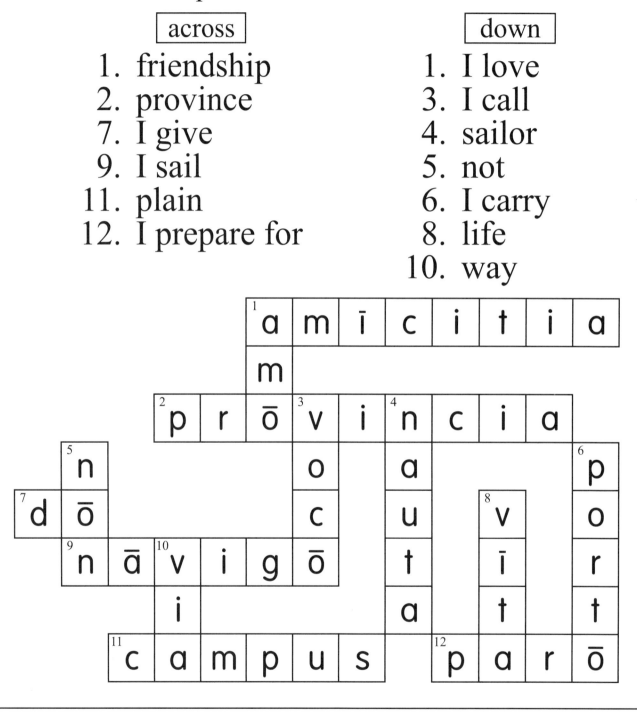

☐ I practiced my flashcards today.

FINAL ALPHABET REVIEW

Write the Latin letters for the sounds.

1. Latin **L l** sounds like **l** in *land*.

2. Latin **Z z** sounds like **dz** in *adze*.

3. Latin **Ā ā** sounds like **a** in *father*.

4. Latin **I i** sounds like **i** in *sit*.

5. Latin **Q q** sounds like **qu** in *quit*.

6. Latin **R r** sounds like **r** in *run*.

7. Latin **Ē ē** sounds like **ey** in *obey*.

8. Latin **Ī ī** sounds like **i** in *machine*.

9. Latin **E e** sounds like **e** in *bet*.

10. Latin **F f** sounds like **f** in *fan*.

☐ I practiced my flashcards today.

FINAL ALPHABET REVIEW

Write the Latin letters for the sounds.

1. Latin **Oo** sounds like **o** in *omit*.
2. Latin **Kk** sounds like **k** in *king*.
3. Latin **Yy** is a shorter sound than **Ȳȳ**.
4. Latin **Bb** sounds like **b** in *boy*.
5. Latin **Ūū** sounds like **u** in *rule*.
6. Latin **Pp** sounds like **p** in *pit*.
7. Latin **Ȳȳ** is a longer sound than **Yy**.
8. Latin **Uu** sounds like **u** in *put*.
9. Latin **Gg** sounds like **g** in *go*.
10. Latin **Dd** sounds like **d** in *dog*.

☐ I practiced my flashcards today.

FINAL ALPHABET REVIEW

Write the Latin letters for the sounds.

1. Latin **Aa** sounds like **a** in *idea*.
2. Latin **Ss** sounds like **s** in *sit*.
3. Latin **Tt** sounds like **t** in *tag*.
4. Latin **Nn** sounds like **n** in *nut*.
5. Latin **Mm** sounds like **m** in *man*.
6. Latin **Ōō** sounds like **o** in *note*.
7. Latin **Cc** sounds like **c** in *cat*.
8. Latin **Xx** sounds like **ks** in *socks*.
9. Latin **Vv** sounds like **w** in *way*.
10. Latin **Hh** sounds like **h** in *hat*.

☐ I practiced my flashcards today.

FINAL DIPHTHONG REVIEW

Write the Latin letters for the sounds.

1. Latin __eu__ sounds like *ay-oo* (in one syllable).

2. Latin __au__ sounds like **ow** in *now*.

3. Latin __ui__ sounds like **uee** in *queen*.

4. Latin __ae__ sounds like *aye*.

5. Latin __oe__ sounds like **oy** in *joy*.

6. Latin __ei__ sounds like **ei** in *neighbor*.

☐ I practiced my flashcards today.

FINAL SPECIAL CONSONANTS REVIEW

Write the Latin letters for the sounds.

1. Latin **gu** sounds like **gu** in *anguish*.

2. Latin **su** sounds like **su** in *suave*.

3. Latin **bs** sounds like *ps*.

4. Latin **i** sounds like **y** in *youth*.

5. Latin **ch** sounds like **ch** in *character*.

6. Latin **ph** sounds like **ph** in *phone*.

7. Latin **th** sounds like **th** in *thick*.

8. Latin **bt** sounds like *pt*.

☐ I practiced my flashcards today.

FINAL VOCABULARY REVIEW

Write the Latin words.

1. I prepare for — parō
2. forest — silva
3. memory — memoria
4. year — annus
5. I fight — pugnō
6. son — fīlius
7. language — lingua
8. territory — ager
9. sailor — nauta
10. and — et

☐ I practiced my flashcards today.

FINAL VOCABULARY REVIEW

Write the Latin words.

1. poet — poēta
2. there are — sunt
3. I like — amō
4. where? — ubi
5. plain — campus
6. girl — puella
7. I capture — occupō
8. island — īnsula
9. I call — vocō
10. I give — dō

☐ I practiced my flashcards today.

FINAL VOCABULARY REVIEW

Write the Latin words.

1. letter — littera
2. I look at — spectō
3. I carry — portō
4. with — cum
5. farmhouse — vīlla
6. there is — est
7. sword — gladius
8. friendship — amīcitia
9. not — nōn
10. trumpet — tuba

☐ I practiced my flashcards today.

FINAL VOCABULARY REVIEW

Write the Latin words.

1. I sail — nāvigō
2. fortune — fortūna
3. but — sed
4. I praise — laudō
5. farmer — agricola
6. gate — porta
7. land — terra
8. woman — fēmina
9. road — via
10. horse — equus

☐ I practiced my flashcards today.

FINAL VOCABULARY REVIEW

Write the Latin words.

1. native land — pātria
2. what? — quid
3. life — vīta
4. friend — amīcus
5. towards — ad
6. province — prōvincia
7. boy — puer
8. water — aqua
9. nature — nātūra
10. daughter — fīlia

☐ I practiced my flashcards today.

APPENDIX

Latin - English Glossary

a
ad - towards or to (51)
ager - field or territory (75)
agricola - farmer (29)
amīcitia - friendship (109)
amīcus - friend (79)
amō - I love or I like (111)
annus - year (119)
aqua - water (31)

c
campus - field or plain (87)
cum - with (91)

d
dō - I give (27)

e
equus - horse (115)
est - he is, she is, it is, there is (33)
et - and (37)

f
fēmina - woman (35)
filia - daughter (105)
filius - son (101)
fortūna - fortune or chance (65)

g
gladius - sword (125)

i
īnsula - island (43)

l
laudō - I praise (47)
lingua - tongue or language (113)
littera - letter (97)

m
memoria - memory (57)

n
nātūra - nature (83)
nauta - sailor (93)
nāvigō - I sail (59)
nōn - not (49)

o
occupō - I seize or I capture (89)

p
parō - I prepare or I prepare for (77)
patria - country or native land (103)
poēta - poet (117)
porta - gate (55)
portō - I carry (69)
prōvincia - province (127)
puella - girl (21)
puer - boy (25)
pugnō - I fight (121)

q
quid - what? (71)

s
sed - but (61)
silva - forest (39)
spectō - I look at (81)
sunt - they are, there are (45)

t
terra - earth or land (123)
tuba - trumpet (73)

u
ubi - where? (99)

v
via - road or way (67)
vīlla - farmhouse (95)
vīta - life (53)
vocō - I call (23)

Note: The number in parentheses indicates the page on which the vocabulary word is introduced.

APPENDIX

English - Latin Glossary

a
and - et
are - sunt

b
boy - puer
but - sed

c
call - vocō
capture - occupō
carry - portō
chance - fortūna
country - patria

d
daughter - fīlia

e
earth - terra

f
farmer - agricola
farmhouse - vīlla
field - ager, campus
fight - pugnō
forest - silva
fortune - fortūna
friend - amīcus
friendship - amīcitia

g
gate - porta
girl - puella
give - dō

h
horse - equus

i
is - est
island - īnsula

l
land - terra
language - lingua
letter - littera
life - vīta
like - amō
look at - spectō
love - amō

m
memory - memoria

n
native land - patria
nature - nātūra
not - nōn

p
plain - campus
poet - poēta
praise - laudō
prepare - parō
prepare for - parō
province - prōvincia

r
road - via

s
sail - nāvigō
sailor - nauta
seize - occupō
son - fīlius
sword - gladius

t
territory - ager
to - ad
tongue - lingua
towards - ad
trumpet - tuba

w
water - aqua
way - via
what? - quid
where? - ubi
with - cum
woman - fēmina

y
year - annus

APPENDIX

Latin Alphabet

Capital Letter	Small Letter	Pronunciation	Capital Letter	Small Letter	Pronunciation
Ā	ā	a in *father*	N	n	n in *nut*
A	a	a in *idea*	Ō**	ō**	o in *note*
B	b	b in *boy*	O**	o**	o in *omit*
C	c	c in *cat*	P	p	p in *pit*
D	d	d in *dog*	Q	q	qu in *quit*
Ē	ē	ey in *obey*	R	r	r in *run*
E	e	e in *bet*	S	s	s in *sit*
F	f	f in *fan*	T	t	t in *tag*
G	g	g in *go*	Ū	ū	u in *rule*
H	h	h in *hat*	U	u	u in *put*
Ī	ī	i in *machine*	V	v	w in *way*
I*	i*	i in *sit*	X	x	ks in *socks*
K	k	k in *king*	Ȳ	ȳ	form lips to say "oo" but say "ee" instead (held longer)
L	l	l in *land*	Y	y	form lips to say "oo" but say "ee" instead (held shorter)
M	m	m in *man*	Z	z	dz in *adze*

*When functioning as a consonant, i has the sound of y in *youth*. (See **Special Consonants** below.)
**The ō and the o both have a long o sound, but the ō is held longer.

Special Sounds

Diphthongs

Letters	Pronunciation
ae	*aye*
au	ow in *now*
ei	ei in *neighbor*
eu	*ay-oo*
oe	oy in *joy*
ui	uee in *queen*

Special Consonants

Letters	Pronunciation
bs	*ps*
bt	*pt*
ch	ch in *character*
gu	gu in *anguish*
i	y in *youth*
ph	ph in *phone*
su	su in *suave*
th	th in *thick*

Latin Workbook - Level 2
Copyright © 1997 by Karen Mohs

APPENDIX

Flashcard Tips

1. Remember to practice flashcards daily.
2. Do not move ahead in the workbook if your student is struggling for mastery. Review the flashcards every day until your student is confident and ready to learn more.